Public Gestures

❦

To Genevieve —

Happy reading & best wishes!

— Matt

Portland, OR 12/26/05

Public Gestures

poems by
Matt Yurdana

UNIVERSITY OF TAMPA PRESS • TAMPA, FLORIDA

Copyright © 2005 by Matt Yurdana. All rights reserved.

Cover art: Detail from *Children's Games* by Pieter Bruegel the Elder. 1560.
Courtesy of Kunsthistorisches Museum, Vienna.

Photograph of the author by Mount Burns. Copyright © 2005 by Mount Burns.

Manufactured in the United States of America
Printed on acid-free paper ∞
First Edition

No part of this book may be reproduced, stored in a retrieval system, or transmitted in any form or by any means, electronic, mechanical, photocopying, recording, or otherwise, except as may be expressly permitted by the applicable copyright statutes or in writing by the publisher.

The University of Tampa Press
401 West Kennedy Boulevard
Tampa, FL 33606

ISBN 1-879852-38-1 (cloth)
ISBN 1-879852-39-X (pbk.)

Browse & order online at
http://utpress.ut.edu

Library of Congress Cataloging-in-Publication Data

Yurdana, Matt.
  Public gestures : poems / by Matt Yurdana.-- 1st ed.
    p. cm.
  ISBN-13: 978-1-879852-38-9 (cloth : alk. paper) ISBN-10: 1-879852-38-1 (cloth : alk. paper)
  ISBN-13: 978-1-879852-39-6 (pbk. : alk. paper) ISBN-10: 1-879852-39-X (pbk. : alk. paper)
  I. Title.
  PS3625.U73P83 2005
  811'.6--dc22   2005018029

Contents

I. Anecdotes

Check-up for the Tattooed Man	3
Accidents, Hemophilia, and Grace	5
And Like Music, the Mouth	9
Degas' Model	12
Dogs and Families	15
Ontogeny	18
Another Variation on Desire	21
Like Giacometti	23
Houdini's Boyhood	25
Death in the Petting Zoo	28

II. Seven Gestures

Shaking Hands	33
Yawning	34
Kneeling	35
Winking	36
Waving	37
Giving the Finger	38
Applauding	39

III. Part Memory

The Unpredictable Lives of Carp	43
My Days with Earl Kessler	46
A Pair of Shoes	49
Yolo County Fair, 1976	51
The Problem with Listening	53
The Dead Whale	55
Killing Salmon	57
Kitchen Window	60
The Pass	62
Meditation on a Hemlock	65
Notes	71
Acknowledgments	73
About the Author	75
About the Book	77

for Jude

*All these things entered you
As if they were both the door and what came through it.*

—Seamus Heaney

I. Anecdotes

Check-up for the Tattooed Man

She holds the stethoscope
near the mouth of a small purple carp

and a faint and muffled murmuring
rises between his third and fourth rib,
spine-deep, so that the sycamores, caged parrots,
and a sun whose rays curl loosely
around his navel, all seem a part of the water
the carp is swimming through.

And again, much louder, under daffodils
at sunrise, beneath a crane's silhouette,
below his left nipple.

There's no way to diagnose
this landscape which is his body,
nothing to prescribe that would make sense
of all she's heard,

but she goes on listening
to the moon with bronchitis, a butterfly
holding hypertension
in its flamboyant wings, until she lifts her hand
and the world goes quiet.

And when she settles again
on his sternum, she's in a forest
where moss is bright green on the north face
of lodgepole pines,

where a lake is a bottomless blue
at the base of steep granite cliffs,
and a red rowboat sits oarless, in last light,
its bow nosing the gravel shore.

When she pushes off
it feels as though the boat is gliding,
her momentum like a magnet
drawn to the center of the lake,

and what was once shoreline is now a thin arc
where trees have fallen into place,
hiding everything behind a beautiful green
that floats over this field of blue,

but even out here she can't ignore
that the water is beating.

Accidents, Hemophilia, and Grace

He tilts upward
in the sudden dim silence under the bus,

feeling the crumpled hood,
the steering column, exposed rods and wires,
all joined in a new configuration
pressing gently against his clothes,

the same tentative pressing, the dragging
of his father's razor across his fingertip,
ten years old, home from the picnic,

almost certain
that he is not like his brother, his fear
as much as the pressure stopping the bleeding.

He can't move
except to turn his head, everywhere
the glass and metal like a skin

just beyond his own skin, and he can't pretend
to know why he isn't dead
anymore than why his grandfather's blood

skipped his father, himself,
but claimed his brother, a simple cut knee
soaking the paper napkins, the blanket,
his father's shirt on the ride to the hospital.

But he does know, did know,
always, even now, some kind of clemency

existing nowhere but inside
his own actions, a calmness that feeds on itself,
a small insanity at the center of his mind.

He marks a woman in the gathering crowd
who shoulders past strangers,

craning and wincing, not wanting but wanting
to find his bloody torso still strapped
firmly in the seat belt,

her mouth forming the word *Jesus*,
while the sirens fade and fire extinguishers
come to him like a distant surf.

He knows she believes
he's received the grace of God,

can see tension in her shoulders,
the same respect and hesitancy his brother has
around glass, machinery, a paring knife,

and he can't deny
that something graceful has occurred,

the beautiful embrace of this twisted dashboard,
the roof hunching as if taking him
into its confidence.

He thinks the world pivots on irony:
the Jaws of Life open; a picnic is reduced
to the relentless blood of an eight year old boy,

and that boy emerges
from the hospital and grows into a man
moving gently, deftly through an ordinary world,
because irony ends in grace,

a thing unexpected that we come to expect
in our fright and arrogance,

as the saw burns through metal
and a makeshift door falls away to late afternoon,

sheets of glass peeled back, a breeze
on his shoulder,

and he raises
his arms for the woman in the crowd,
smiling and waving.

And Like Music, the Mouth

Chopin's nocturne in C-sharp minor, no. 20,
from the tape deck of a stranded taxi
on a dirt road in Malaysia, the driver lugging
a bald spare from the trunk, a warm rain
spattering the banana leaves, his sleeve
through the open window,

and again, in Oregon, in a supermarket,
he heard it near the soups and hot sauces
as he fumbled a jar of pickles
that slowly, finally, burst on the tile floor.

That something so beautiful brings back
the simplest things: taxis, warm rain, broken glass,
makes him think that behind our every action
and even our smallest thoughts,
there is music.

Even now, the same nocturne
as he leans back in the dentist's chair,
Dr. Lazlo probing his upper bicuspids,
while the piano goes *andante*, and a plastic tube
dangles like a hook, sucking
his left cheek dry.

And he believes, like Dr. Lazlo, that the mouth
is the body's greatest contradiction,
both solid and pliant, obtuse and vulnerable,
because he himself is a dentist,

has contemplated thousands
of mouths and found that they are always
more than themselves, like music,
heightening, summing up, revealing:
the immaculate woman with advanced gingivitis,
or the casual, muscular men who lean back,
refuse Novocain, then go pale and sweaty
at the sound of the drill.

And like music, the mouth
is surrounded by pain, day in and day out,
though it has become so familiar
he can't feel it.

But now he stares into Dr. Lazlo's glasses
and finds small slender fingers,
a delicate probe, an angled mirror,
all in the tiny reflection of his own mouth.
He watches the tip of the instrument
push beneath his gum line,

and he opens wider,
following its path over each tooth,
anticipating every move,
at once watching and working on himself,

so when the probe slips between his molars
he's ready for the pain a moment
before it happens, eyes already closed, his hands
gripping the armrests, the piano leading
and Dr. Lazlo humming along.

Degas' Model

He remembers turning fourteen the summer he sat
for *Nude Boy in Morning Light*;

"A lesser painting," the docent says,
"but a good example of the dusky interiors
that preceded the brighter, fresher hues
more in-line with Impressionism."

The German couple nods encouragingly,
mindful of their cameras, and a woman squints,
tilts her head, so hushed and attentive,
steeping herself until she not only sees and hears
but *understands* that summer morning,

while the docent unfolds a small metal wand
and points to the brush work
along the declivity of his lower back.

He felt a breeze on his shoulders,
the patio doors ajar, while his pale legs
went numb on the red satin cloth,
and from the corner of his eye a corner
of the easel and a battered tin, from which Edgar

(he had insisted on being called Edgar)
produced the dusty plums he loathed.

No, not the plums, but the chewing and swallowing,
the pause before the next bite.

For this seemed the epitome of summer:
days as fleeting as fruit, but within those days
an unbearable lingering,

with Edgar savoring his plums, his brush
poised over the canvas, watching
for some alignment, or inference, or change of light
in that dim parlor the docent compares
with Caravaggio.

What he suffered was more painful
than restlessness, sharper than puberty,
as he sat aching on the red satin cloth,

but he steps forward, squints, tilts his head,
and can't decide if what he remembers
is his own misery or the misery Edgar remembered,

or a misery so commonplace it has lost
its texture, like the body of morning light,
and is only recognized in paintings.

"Not misery," the docent says,
"but the slender moment before desire."
And he nods and agrees.

Dogs and Families

Every April, his brother's arthritic dog rises
with the first daffodils, and sets off
from the shallow dusty trough under the front porch,
the season like an ointment he wears to wander
the back lots, weedy culverts, and compost piles
his condition has denied him.

And he begins to eat things,
forgetting taste and appetite, his hunger
gaining momentum, pulling him along
until he devours what other dogs only mark or sniff,
and bears it all home in his sagging belly
like answers to the question of his wanderings,
answers his brother can't understand, but tries, each April,
to find some pattern or progression or story
from their ghostly outlines in the vet's X-ray:
two sparkplugs, nine AA batteries, a bottle of Listerine,
his neighbor's slippers, a pair of panty hose.

His brother tells him this only hours
after his own dog has died, while they sit in a diner
eating pie and drinking coffee.

And only his brother, he thinks, would choose
this anecdote instead of condolences, this lunatic dog

a comfort for his suffering, or the strange hunger
a metaphor for some deep-seated insecurity;
or perhaps it means they now share something in common,
some bewildered fondness for the ways of dogs
though they have lived in the same town for years
and never shared a thing but these occasional painful meals
which they will never give up; even now, his brother
spilling his coffee while insisting on the bill,
proving that for each gesture of kindness
there is an equal and opposite action that keeps his family
circling but never reaching one another.

He remembers the first dog
the two of them ever owned, a dachshund-terrier mix
their father brought home to teach the meaning
of commitment.

And at first it was enough, commitment
like a scaffolding from which they built their obsession,
each bowl of food or walk around the neighborhood
as intimate as a whisper, and what they whispered
at night was the dog's future, one day at a time,
taken from all the days before,
until finally it was not enough, and one afternoon
they carried the dog out to the garage
with an old blanket and the egg timer from the kitchen.

And he realizes now that even then
he was learning how to lose, though at the time
it felt like love, a love so clear and fulfilling
it could forgive all the ignorance inside of them,
as they set the timer for thirty minutes
and laid the dog down in the storage freezer between
the frozen peas and Cornish game hens
and imagined the tenderness, the sweet moment
of the dog's rescue.

Even now he can feel it, while they argue
over the bill, mopping up coffee with their napkins:
the two of them still waiting.

Ontogeny

For seven years
Doris has dissected cecropia moths,

extracting hormones
from the reddish powdery heads
pinned in rows on the wax tablets.

She is pretty like a moth.
Her hands feather over the probes
and tiny scalpels,

testing a genetic pesticide which confuses
the moth's molting pattern,

so that they blunder after adolescence,
short-winged larvae wobbling
and fighting their own bodies.

Three months since her husband's cancer
and Doris still swims at midnight
in Lake Vasona. She leaves

the silent house, walking
under red alders and yellow streetlights,

her shadow pulling
from each bright spot into darkness,

and buys vodka
from Harry's 24-hour market
where a young man from the college
hovers and asks what she studies.

He hears her say *math*, and drifts off
glaring at his shoes,

and Doris understands him,
like moths quivering
against the neon beer signs,
like the pull of hormones,

and her husband's hands unsteady
on her breasts, as if brittle panes of glass
formed the husks of their bodies.

Tonight she is guided by sounds,
the abrupt silence of crickets
in the hydrangea, mallards gabbling over

a field of clover, under thin bright stars
clear as vodka.

She can hear the whole lake shifting
the old cans and small pebbles,

and her limbs gleam against the limbs
of oaks, clothes strewn
in the dry grass, stepping into water
that receives her.

Each day moves like this,
she thinks, the steady pull of crickets
until dawn,

and pushing through darkness
which is both now and tomorrow

and buoyant,
only the sound of breathing,
fingers going numb,

the moon floating on her belly.

Another Variation on Desire

The menu just opened, the table smelling of vinegar,

and a man talking about hunting geese as a boy, lying beside
   his father before dawn
in a field of winter wheat, beneath a makeshift blanket of old
   burlap sacks,
poised for the distant honking and the rush of a thousand
   wings,

and in the held breath of that sunrise his friend
calls for help, and looking two booths back I see the cook
   already kneeling
beside him, his ear an inch from the man's mouth;

then my fingers against the quiet of his neck, unbuttoning
the mother-of-pearl buttons on his flannel shirt, and how his
   sternum is the pattern,

shallow as a footprint in sand, of the heel of my hand,
and the pattern of my counting weaving unrehearsed
through the before and after of the cook's blowing, through
   the rise and fall
of the waitress on the phone with 911, the tempo of our
   stopgap momentum

in his billowing cheeks, his rib cage springing back,
in the strange new clock our hands and lungs have become,
   minute by minute,
until there's no past or future, no moment
but this moment my counting creates, and continues,

unbroken under the sirens and lights, ignoring the airbag
and the whine of the defibrillator, a rhythm that stops for
   nothing,
not even the hand on my shoulder.

Like Giacometti

She can smell the damp clay of her hair
his fingers built and rebuilt hours ago, and hours before that,
while sometimes he wept, sometimes splintering a chair
against a wall,

like Matisse cursing his blue nude, or like Cézanne
who, it is said, heaved his self-portrait from a studio window.

And like Giacometti, he only sculpts what he remembers,
no model, no sketches, and lately no lights,
because even light is distracting, so that he wears dark glasses
in his dim studio, working the bust he has shaped
in her likeness,

and she reaches out as he has reached out
since they first met, cupping her jaw line, a finger
worrying the rim of her ear, the scar
on her chin from that first summer with roller skates,
smooth like the bell of a tiny trumpet.

Where did this come from, this moment
that is the focus of so much weeping and broken furniture?

The wrinkles at the corners of her eyes
mean she was looking up, perhaps late afternoon, the sun
just over his shoulder,

her head tilting as it does when she is waiting,
listening for a thing she can almost hear, an idea, a thought,
before it is voiced after eating or making love
or walking to the supermarket, feeling
the contentment and guilt of knowing what he will say
before he says it.

And all this he has captured, but somehow forgotten
she was smiling.

Houdini's Boyhood

He slips from the house, no lights,
an hour before dawn,

the world taking the shape of sounds,

his footfall
on the graveled levee,

and farther,
the only streetlight in town
buzzing from red to green,

and beyond that, a rising squall
which is the great flocks of geese
waking in Delmer's alfalfa.

At the water's edge,
he crawls
under an old refrigerator box
disguised with mud,
cattails, long limp strands of tule.

He has seen hunters lie down
in the fields of young winter wheat,
hidden with netting

and old burlap
an hour before first light,
the frost melting under their bodies,

as if they waited beneath
the landscape,

geese wheeling at daybreak
over the field they had become.

And now hundreds arrive,
surround him,
the yelping and straining wings
from every spring morning of his life,

as light slowly defines
the one small hole that allows the marsh in.

Everything he learns, he learns
in darkness,
the long painful crouching,
to balance his weight with his toes.

His breath is shallow and silent
in the middle of these birds

that preen and squabble
into a new day, nudging the cardboard,

and he is convinced
he is not here.

Death in the Petting Zoo

His toupee shifted in the breeze;
a Nigerian goat chewed the leg of his trousers;
but only at closing did we realize he'd been there all along,
on a bench beside the llamas, with an empty bag
of alfalfa pellets and a red balloon tied to his wrist.

Perhaps he was almost asleep, believing himself awake,
watching a young girl feed chocolate cake
to a pot-bellied pig; it was her birthday, her friends
in party hats dashing through the pens, upsetting the animals,
and he dreamed he went to the pig's rescue,
taking it in his arms, hopping the fence, walking on
past the cheetahs, the aviary, clearing the park's entrance
in search of good clean farmland, while the children
giggled and the girl gently tied the balloon around his wrist
as a prank he would never wake from.

Or maybe the balloon was there from the start,
signal to a blind date, or a lover, or a son whose turn it was
to spend the weekend with his father,
and though he had pictures (we found them in his wallet)
he knew they were only gross approximations,
his son almost teenage, almost within reach, outgrowing
their weekends together before they began,
as he watched the peafowl pacing the fence line,

stepping carefully in their own droppings like old men
trying to navigate a frozen sidewalk, and he wondered
for the last time: *how long did it take these birds
to forget they have wings.*

Perhaps he'd wandered in by accident,
or maybe he'd planned it for weeks, to be surrounded
by the sweet dusty manure, the sweetness of children
touching animals, the last things which become our first
   things,
these small details pointing back toward his life,
because no matter who he was on all the days before,
or how many rumors we invent to understand
whatever killed him, we can imagine none of it
without the red balloon.

II. Seven Gestures

Shaking Hands

It is *successful*, he thinks, for lack of a better word,

a reflexive, pleasant, well-balanced joining of the public sides
of two selves, the tongue and groove
of every honest welcome he has ever known,

but sometimes it is, like this evening, too much or not enough,
misaligned between the thumb and forefinger, the palm, the wrist;

a stumbling or a jockeying at the leading edge
of this first impression, this soft, almost-hot hand of an old
   friend
of his wife,

and the way he comes at it sideways, holding on
a moment too long, his elbow crooked out away from his body
suggests the eagerness of compensation,

not for a particular mistake, not a lie or a bribe, or even
an old affair with his wife,

but something deep and sustained this handshake has pointed to
like a compass, for which he will never forgive him.

Yawning

Never more than a moment's warning,
and never a choice in the matter, though he tries
choosing not to, pitting himself against his own jaws;

but whether he stifles it, or succumbs
completely and unconditionally

there's no way that his boss,
who's in the middle of recounting his weekend in Jackson
   Hole,
will ever believe it was anything but the briefest glimpse
of the most honest moment between them.

Kneeling

She's poised in the center of her mother's sweeping,
palms down, head bowed, a loose strand of hair touching the
   floorboards
as lightly as the broom answering her,

poised between conviction and uncertainty
and the quick, almost-anger of having become, in one
   gesture,
so willingly vulnerable,

like the first few moments of a prayer, when an answer
still seems important.

Winking

Between two converging waiters,
the unfolding of a menu,
and a maze of arms and glasses of Merlot,

she receives it, holds it for a moment
in her steady and unreadable eyes
before turning away,

and given her composure
this seems to him a tiny invitation
to convince himself that although he can't see
her face, she is smiling.

Waving

She wants to believe
it's timid, not hesitant,

like the first line crossed in a long line
of commitments, a gesture that might someday
remind her of the word *love*,

somewhere beyond the tips of his fingertips,
or how his palm seems to cup the shape
of her chin, or the profile of his wrist bone,
no bigger than a bee sting, the way it is the piece missing
from the small of her back,

but here he is again, the last one off the plane,
holding nothing but air.

Giving the Finger

It's the wrong animal
to shoulder so much anger and attitude,

this small flightless bird hovering
in the hands of football fans,
on playgrounds, at the movies, after every word
has already been said between lovers,

even perched above the sun roof
of a car merging into traffic, in lieu of a blinker,
shaking a little for emphasis,
so slender and awkward it's hard to believe it means
what the driver wants it to mean,
like being threatened with a butter knife.

Applauding

It was, among many things, Fernando's eyebrows:

their little archways of surprise just wide enough
for indignation,

and their softness—unlike the elaborate furrowing
of the woman who played the detective—making him
almost attractive,

and the way he didn't use them at all
in the third act, after he'd killed the doctor,

the calmness they conveyed as he looked downstage
with the ball peen hammer still in his hands.

He is brilliant, she thinks, and his brilliance
sweetens as the cast takes a final bow, his eyebrows
nearly touching with humility and gratitude
in the match-flare of applause

that flickers from hand to hand until the moment
is like a flame divided;

Fernando is its beautiful fuel, and she is the appetite.

III. Part Memory

The Unpredictable Lives of Carp

On the ninth day of rain, the Japanese maple came unmoored,
asters dimpled the surface, lobelias spun through an archipelago
  of vegetable beds as the sudden streamlets
scoured the landscaping, sculpting it, funneling it down into the
  perfect
ear-shaped bowl of the Jorgensens' carp pond.

And the carp rose, all nineteen of them, riding upwellings thick
  with fertilizer and decorative bark,

beaching and floundering along the brickwork, some by the
  potted zinnias,
others in the shallows beneath the African daisies, a tail slap or two
before settling into the stillness of the blossoms around them,
  except the mottled one, the one Mr. Jorgensen picked
for the serious black spot perched above its mouth;

it spilled headlong as if it had always known restlessness, the
  impatience
of rivers, the slap and dash of brooks, shooting the runnels under
  sword ferns and hostas or leaping,
like a would-be salmon, over the mossy hummock beside the
  hydrangea;

it was as bold and reckless as the makeshift falls it followed
    down the length of the terraced yard,
threading the patio furniture, rushing in and out of planter
    boxes
with the flotsam of trellis twine and old seed packages, and
    when it reached the lowest point in the yard

it flew, over the overwhelmed drainage system, arcing on a
    weedy flume
across the narrow alleyway, down into the tar-slick pool
    collecting on the Lipinskis' rooftop.

And there it lived, sustained by the rains, and roof moss, and
    the weekly hatches of mayflies.

It glided under the eastbound clouds, sucked at the surface of
    the last days of spring,
and on into June kept up a watery thrashing through the
    shallow hours
between midnight and dawn, growing strange and muscular at
    the confluence of moonlight and the dreams
rising from Timmy Lipinski's bedroom;

finning at the edges of the night light, claiming each silhouette as
 its own mottled shadow,
even now, twenty years later, Tim can hear it, sloshing toward him
 through the darkness and the wind in the trees.

My Days with Earl Kessler

I believe the rumors, flaring then dying,
week after week, like matches
held up to Earl Kessler
as we pack frozen salmon in the cold room
at Phoenix Seafood.

Earl wears a thick purple sock
on the stump that is his left arm,
a small pendulum we measure the day by.
The rest he lost

without anesthetics, only boot laces
and a machete on the border
of northern Laos,

or a few wrong inches
after 12 hours with a hay baler
on a farm in Nevada,

or the time he gouged a man's eyes
with that single crooked thumb,

or the one I almost believe,
that he was mauled
by three Dobermans and a pit bull

on his mother's 35th birthday,
stumbling into the house, holding
what was left of his elbow
as she was blowing out the candles.

There are moments before
the morning shift, when Earl and the rest of us
might talk, but instead we sit

on the hulls of overturned skiffs,
drinking coffee, watching the net menders
spooling mounds of herring web,

and no horizon beyond the docks,
no imprint in the fog dividing
sky from water, rows of boats
adrift on the air.

By 10 a.m. a line will appear,
a seam joining two fields of gray, gulls
balanced near the curve of the earth,

and by 2 p.m. the islands, the bow pickers
with their own outlines,

like a foothold, like a moth resting
on the whiteness of a ceiling.

At 7 p.m. I emerge, numb and blinking,
from the smell of fish
I've long since stopped smelling,

the boats sitting their own reflections
in the last light of day.

And I'll walk the half mile upstream
through bogs and willow thickets,
to a small meadow where I've heard

Earl sometimes sits,
shirtless in the weakening light,
straddling a dead log,
his head, shoulders, and ruined arm
covered with bread crumbs,

and a flock of chickadees
falling and rising from his body.

A Pair of Shoes

The juggler implores and we respond with a wine glass,
two wristwatches, someone's Louis L'Amour novel, each
    joining the cascade and replacing, one by one,
the turquoise clubs now littering the lawn.

Like all crowds we begin with the urge to confound him with
    bowling balls or bristling Swiss Army knives,
but the ease with which he knows, immediately, the heft and
    angle
of each object, the essential spin or necessary arc, wins us over,
    until we believe
in the return of a set of keys momentarily lost
in the leaves overhead, or that he can retrieve a pair of
    sunglasses from the center of the sun;

and there are a few of us who see his juggling as one long
    vertiginous analogy,

like the woman who steps forward and reaches up the back of
    her shirt, unclasps her bra,
and slides it, like a magician's scarf, from her left sleeve
then makes a loose ball and lobs it, watches it trade places
    with an instamatic camera, as the pattern becomes
a fountain in which it emerges again and again like a bright
    coin.

Inspired, I offer up my shoes with a lazy heel-over-toe pitch,
laces flailing as they're caught up in this momentum
that carries a dog's collar and a cell phone ascending on its
   first ring, that buoys the bra and keeps
the wine glass half full, regardless of its crazy spinning.

And though my shoes are dancing a dance impossible to
   choreograph,
there's something familiar in the way they arch overhead that
   reminds me of my own lopsidedness,
my own slight shuffling with every toss, yet lighter, less
   graceless,
as if these shoes remember the bravado that dancing can bring
   on, a stand-in for talent,

like that heady confidence when Cheryl Bellafonte said yes
at my first high school dance, buoying me on our long walk
   under spinning lights to the center of the floor, where we
   turned
to face each other, her hand on my shoulder, mine at her
   waist,
both of us staring at our shoes through the whole first song,
   then laughing, then never looking back.

Yolo County Fair, 1976

We'd broken free,

a backfire on the Tilt-O-Whirl, or a few ill-timed fireworks
springing us from the little corral of trampled dung and sawdust,
    and with my fingers woven into his mane, my knees
pressed to his musky withers, we were a startled breath, a
    shared reflex
as we threaded the parking lot and bolted through acres of
    young alfalfa.

His name was Starlight; he smelled of disinfectant and
    ancient popcorn
and years of exhaust in shadowy trailers; his black eyes
glinted like the little diamonds tooled into his saddle and
    harness, and his hoof beats echoed off the stucco walls
as we cantered through a bedroom community,

striding between station wagons, over lawn gnomes, and
    down
into an empty labyrinth of identical floor plans and cul-de-sacs,
as if on a path rutted into the tight canyons of his brain that
    no asphalt or landscaping could conceal.

And his eyes were my eyes, his gait my confidence and the
    swinging in my stomach, our leggy shadow trailing us

uphill along the sweep of an avenue lined with mailboxes
where I reached down into each one, gathering a great pile
   between me
and the saddle horn, then shucked them open,

bills fluttering like ponderous leaves, coupons catching along
   the shrubberies, keeping only
a sweepstakes winner, a car magazine, and a letter from
   someone named Rose,
not more than a paragraph, the postmark from Tempe,
   Arizona;
I hope you're happy, she wrote, *because you've now got everything
   you asked for.*
Good luck.

The Problem with Listening

At a time like this, he's simply helpless, his ears
like two little wells the world wishes in,

brimming with the first ingredients for Cajun tapenade,
three reasons to never buy a Ford, a cough and a sigh,
and somewhere near the restrooms the headlong sincerity
of a father explaining escrow to his son;

all this, while his girlfriend deliberates, a finger sculpting
the foam of her cappuccino, perfectly content to be
the only one in this café he can't hear.

If he's lucky, she thinks that he, too, is poised
on the edge of discussion,

but a man is unhappy with his washing machine
while one woman convinces another that a new haircut
might accentuate her cheekbones;

baseball scores, a back-handed compliment,
the polite but growing impatience with the new cashier,
and some kind of fight three tables over, every third word
an island above the whispering,

and above it all, Billie Holiday playing devil's advocate
in that sleepy, nonchalant way that reminds him
of his mother's humming when he was a boy,
Saturday mornings, summertime, the smell of pancakes:

my life a hell you're making
you know I'm yours just for the taking,

and he nods, studies the tabletop, strokes his chin
because he realizes that she's spoken and he's missed it,
her eyes saying ten, maybe fifteen seconds
before this silence lasts days, maybe a week,

leaving him no choice but to bet it all on what he thinks
is most probable, most dangerous; he smiles,
looks her in the eye, then says *yes.*

The Dead Whale

The two of them nearly in love, raising and lowering their
    clothes, taking inventory of scars:

the three-inch arabesque from a box cutter, a fishing hook's
    ghostly dimple,
the palest appendectomy just above the bikini line,
and glass remembered everywhere, on fingers, shoulder
    blades, a little peppering on both knees, a shallow *S*
along the left instep from a walk on the beach,

and the one like a thumbprint she calls *an indelible history*,
    and the one he's named *the shortest distance between
    mistakes*.

They catalog the length and breadth and beyond, even the
    nicks and cuts, the traumas and past surgeries
they hold dearly but can't claim as their own:
the cat's abscess, the dog's dramatic neutering, the C-sections,
    now light as watermarks, they both rose from,

and after the initials on trees and the name carved for two
    weeks
into the wood of a seventh-grade desk top, they sit down to a
    PBS documentary on the life of whales,

where an adult Humpback has died in open water and the
    narrator follows
the camera's slow tour past every scar: strange abrasions,
    echoes of teeth marks,
the crenulated one-time home of crustaceans, and the faintest
    trailings, like scrimshaw along the dorsal ridge,

what the narrator calls *the Devil's calligraphy,* each one an
    explanation, a reason written in the clarity of the moment
but not enough, alone or together, to finish the story.

Killing Salmon

After five weeks it's difficult to see them, each like a shadow
   with the same struggle and heft as the one it follows,

the swift, tapered moments nearly overlapping

as we wade into them, in pairs, after the net is pulled taut,
   one of us stooping to find the muscled groove above the tail
   that's made for the hand,

then twisting it up while sliding thumb and forefinger inside
   the gills, holding it out and away from the body, while the
   other

delivers two quick blows behind the eyes with a length of steel
   pipe, a shuddering, then a deep loosening

as it rides the conveyor up to the spawning room.

Those first days, their dramatic humps, the reds and bruised
   greens moving like a thunderstorm across their bellies

kept us respectful and arrogant, believing we were an essential
   link in their life cycle,

but now, every third day or so, one of us slips into a
   rage; maybe it's a blunt snout ramming his shin, or the
   overgrown teeth snagging his waders

that makes him climb, as each of us has climbed, the cement
   bank of the holding pond, dragging the salmon behind him
   with more anger

than long hours, miserable pay, and the agony of our lower
   backs should allow,
fifteen seconds where everything wrong in his life exists in the
   body of this fish,

and he kneels, jaws clenched, ears gone red, swinging the steel
   pipe again and again until it is unrecognizable;

and afterward, before his breathing slows, he tries to tell
   himself he didn't enjoy it, that it wasn't satisfying, but back
   in the pond

he's a little embarrassed, a little afraid, and it lingers

like the nightmares he used to wake from on those summer
   nights from back home,

trembling in the bathroom, washing his face under the
   startling light or catching the tail end of an old black and
   white late-night movie,

where two lovers suffered over a whisper out of context, a
   letter in the wrong hands, a message never delivered on
   which the entire plot rests,

simple and reassuring, mistakes he'd made a dozen times,
   misunderstandings he could understand and carry with him
   back into sleep.

Kitchen Window

Washing dishes, he sees what she's worked so hard to keep
 hidden;
twenty yards away, framed by her kitchen window, she reaches
 behind the dusty china on the topmost shelf

and takes two long nips from a metal flask while her son's
 busy clearing the table,
the slightest, most practiced pause from routine
before she scours a pan, refrigerates the milk, wraps something
 that looks like chicken;

but her drinking's so quick he can't be certain
that what he saw wasn't a small shiny glass masquerading as
 a flask, not hiding but resting momentarily on the topmost
 shelf,
a few, innocent, well-deserved ounces at the end of a long
 day;

so he dries his silverware and watches her clean,
a general busyness with the dish towel that could easily double
 as a kind of camouflage, or anxiety, or a lack of control that
 belies the way she checks and rechecks
the seal on each piece of Tupperware,

though she seems so *in control*, not a hint of over-compensation
while she laughs and dishes up the ice cream, and if the flask
   is anywhere it is deep in the shadows

on the topmost shelf of her mind, guiding, however gently,
   her briefest thoughts, her smallest decisions,

so that now the day's restraints fade as the light fades and
   evening comes down
to eclipse every distraction keeping her from her drink,
though watching her now it's ridiculous to think so, and just
   as he decides to doubt it all,

she turns, taking his certainty and the two bowls of ice cream
and leaving him a glimpse of the stove, a half-moon view of
   the clock on her wall, the sliver of a doorway,
beyond which there are no more assumptions, only her son,
   who, chances are, already knows, has known for years.

The Pass

We stand in a circle, comparing sunburn stories while the
   snowplow re-creates the pass
and our cars sit buried to their hubcaps;

passionate burns, illicit burns, all those patterns that signaled
where we went beyond where we usually draw the line, and
   one guy who tells of falling asleep on a rooftop after making
   love,
whose girlfriend wrote *BLISS* in sunscreen on his back, visible
   for weeks;

stories like the stories around a scar,
with just enough inaccuracy to help others think of us the way
   we'd like them to.

And today, too, is a story, how we arrange our sudden
   camaraderie,
or claim the beginnings of frostbite, or tack a few hours onto
   the time we sit stranded,
and how natural, how selfless we are, moving without thinking
toward the woman flagging us from the Garden City Pet Store
   van.

The van's heater is broken, so she kneels before the cages with
    a hair dryer,
waving it in large sweeping arcs, pausing a little longer over
    the reptiles, but the animals are motionless,
noses under tails, heads under wings, hunching or balling
    themselves around what must feel like sleep.

And when she begs us to take them, to drive as many animals
    as we can to the pet store in the valley below, no one
    hesitates;
we make promises, write directions and the phone number on
    the backs of our hands,
then stand in a line beside the van's door, ready for whatever
    we're handed:

an African gray and a bowl of hermit crabs goes to the woman
    with the Camaro,
two ferrets and three fire-bellied toads for the retired couple
    from Billings,
and the guy who fell asleep on the rooftop
walks off with a young whippet, a skink, and a pair of peach-
    faced love birds cradled in his oversized mittens.

I hold out my arms, and she hands me a spectacled caiman,
three and a half feet long, writhing in slow-motion, its yellow-
  green scales surreal against the snow I'm now running
  through,

back to my car, and it might not die if I'm fast enough, if I
  can just crank up the heater,
remove my jacket, unbutton my shirt to its cold plated belly
  while its teeth rest gently against my neck;
if I can pull it off, this is how I'll begin.

Meditation on a Hemlock

Twice today, I've returned to the hemlock
and run my fingers along the small twin teeth marks.

It's a skinny tree, four fingers wide, prominent
along this bank of chewed stumps, and having lost

the other trees, it seems less of a tree itself,
more like a guidepost visible from half a mile down river,

branches dripping quietly, so green and all alone
I can't ignore these teeth marks.

What stopped the beaver from gnawing it down?
And what keeps him from coming back?

So many beautiful implications circling the hemlock:
the wind, the tides, the clouds of black flies,

and although each one is of little consequence
this doesn't stop me from trying to explain

not only this tree, but the whole mountainside,
the way it makes no difference

if God created each link in the world,
or we have created Him, because the impulse is the same.

I remember walking down Montgomery street,
twelve years old, one of the few clear summer days

in San Francisco when the sun was everywhere,
in shop windows and the chrome of parked cars.

A woman in a green dress stepped out
onto a balcony ahead of me, holding a fish bowl,

and tossed it over the railing as she might have tossed
bread to a pond full of ducks, the water sloshing

then ribboning off the lip, the colored gravel rising,
pulling away from the goldfish that swam up

through air and water and sunlight, dropping between
telephone lines, flashing in the path of a blackbird,

so that in its moment of falling, everything
that didn't belong in the bowl belonged.

And as I kneeled in the glass, cupping
the fish in my hands, I didn't know if what I saw

was grief or rage or sweetness in the woman's face,
but I wanted her to do it again.

Notes

Cover: Pieter Bruegel the Elder is considered one of the greatest Flemish painters of the sixteenth century. Many of his paintings have an encyclopedic view of various actions linked by a unifying theme. *Children's Games* shows two hundred and thirty children absorbed in ninety different games. The painting is from the collection of the Kunsthistorisches Museum, Vienna, and is reproduced here by permission of the museum.

Page 51: Yolo County is located in the Central Valley in northern California. *Yolo* is derived from a native Poewin Indian word meaning "abounding in the rushes."

Page 53: "The Problem with Listening" contains an excerpt from "Body and Soul," written by Edward Heyman, John Green, Bob Sour, and Frank Eyton, ©WB Music Corp., Range Road Music, Inc./Quartet Music, Inc. (ASCAP) and Druropetal Music (BMI).

Acknowledgments

My thanks to the editors of the following publications in which these poems first appeared:

    Alaska Quarterly Review: "Meditation on a Hemlock"
    Beloit Poetry Journal: "The Pass"
    The Laurel Review: "Dogs and Families"
    The Massachusetts Review: "Shaking Hands," "Waving,"
        "Giving the Finger"
    The North American Review: "Killing Salmon"
    Poetry Northwest: "Houdini's Boyhood," "My Days with
        Earl Kessler," "Ontogeny"
    Prairie Schooner: "Check-up for the Tattooed Man,"
        "And Like Music, the Mouth"
    River City: "Death in the Petting Zoo"
    The Southern Review: "Accidents, Hemophilia, and Grace"
    Willow Springs: "Like Giacometti"

"Killing Salmon" also appears in *The Pushcart Prize XXVII: Best of the Small Presses, 2003*, Bill Henderson, editor (Wainscott, NY: Pushcart Press); "Giving the Finger" appeared on the Web site *Poetry Daily*, in 2004.

My thanks to Literary Arts, Inc., for the C. Hamilton Bailey Fellowship, which helped support the writing of this book.

Many thanks to Robert Wrigley, Pattiann Rogers, Claire Davis, and George Estreich for their encouragement and guidance on many of these poems. Thanks to Martha Serpas for championing the book. And thanks to Richard Mathews at the University of Tampa Press for his keen eye and untiring enthusiasm.

Finally, my love to Judi Maxey, who makes it all possible.

About the Author

Matt Yurdana has worked at a variety of jobs, including raising salmon at a remote hatchery in Alaska's Prince William Sound, teaching literature to U.S. soldiers near the demilitarized zone in South Korea., and directing a graduate program in creative writing. His poems appear in a variety of journals, including *Alaska Quarterly Review, The Massachusetts Review, The North American Review, Poetry Northwest, Prairie Schooner,* and *The Southern Review.* Among his awards are a Pushcart Prize, the Richard Hugo Memorial Scholarship and the Academy of American Poets Award from the University of Montana, and the C. Hamilton Bailey Fellowship from Oregon Literary Arts. He lives with his wife and two children in Portland, Oregon.

About the Book

Public Gestures is set in Adobe Garamond Pro types based on the sixteenth century roman types of Claude Garamond and the complementary italic types of Robert Granjon. They were adapted for digital composition by Robert Slimbach in consultation with colleagues including type historian and designer Steven Harvard, letterform expert John Lane, and Adobe's Fred Brady. Slimbach and Brady have written that Garamond's "roman types are arguably the best conceived typefaces ever designed, displaying a superb balance of elegance and practicality." The book was designed and typeset by Richard Mathews at the University of Tampa Press with a cover design in collaboration with Matt Yurdana. It has been printed on acid-free text papers, with printing and binding by Fidlar Doubleday of Kalamazoo, Michigan.

Poetry from the University of Tampa Press

Jenny Browne, *At Once*

Richard Chess, *Chair in the Desert*

Richard Chess, *Tekiah*

Kathleen Jesme, *Fire Eater*

Lance Larsen, *In All Their Animal Brilliance**

Julia B. Levine, *Ask**

Sarah Maclay, *Whore**

John Willis Menard, *Lays in Summer Lands*

Jordan Smith, *For Appearances**

Lisa M. Steinman, *Carslaw's Sequences*

Marjorie Stellmach, *A History of Disappearance*

Richard Terrill, *Coming Late to Rachmaninoff*

Matt Yurdana, *Public Gestures*

* *Denotes winner of the Tampa Review Prize for Poetry*